UNCONTAINABLE
NOISE

Winner of the 2004-05 Transcontinental Poetry Award

UNCONTAINABLE
NOISE

July 17, 2009

For John Burnside, whose words
are anything but noise. Here's hoping
we meet next year at Allison's.
If LIES ABOUT MY FATHER had come out
a few years earlier, I would have

STEVE DAVENPORT

stolen Mrs. Donaldson's line from it —
"It's hard work, being happy." — and
put it in this book. (See page 69.)

your fan,

Steve Davenport

PAVEMENT SAW PRESS
OHIO

Editor & Layout : David Baratier
Associate Editor: Sean Karns
Duck Logo: Joe Napora
Cover art: Angela Y. Lee
Author Photo: Richard Powers

Acknowledgments: Some of the poems were published in earlier forms and under different titles in the following places: *580 Split, Another Chicago Magazine, Chachalaca Poetry Review, CutBank, Faultline, Flyway, The Iowa Review, Lilies and Cannonballs, Many Mountains Moving, Pavement Saw, Rhino, Sou'wester, Talking River Review, Thin Air Magazine.*

"Up From The Wreck Conjuring Montana Sonnet" was anthologized in *Red, White, & Blues: Poetic Vistas on the Promise of America.* (Virgil Suarez and Ryan Van Cleave, eds. U of Iowa P, 2004.)

Pavement Saw Press
PO Box 6291
Columbus, OH 43206
pavementsaw.org

Ohio Arts Council
A STATE AGENCY
THAT SUPPORTS PUBLIC
PROGRAMS IN THE ARTS

Products are available through the publisher or through:
SPD / 1341 Seventh St. / Berkeley, CA 94710 / 510.524.1668

Winner of the 2004-05 Transcontinental Poetry Award for an outstanding first book-length collection of poetry or prose. We read yearly from June 1st until August 15th. Send SASE for information.

CONTENTS

TWENTY YODELS

O'KEEFFE AND STEVENS

ANOTHER YODEL

ALL THIS TUG

LAST YODEL

for Lynn,
for Family

Meanwhile W. S. in his suit
is thinking chaos is thinking fences.
In his head--the seeds of fresh pain
his exorcising,
the bellow of locked blood.

—Michael Ondaatje,
"King Kong Meets Wallace Stevens"

TWENTY YODELS

ARRANGE THEIR SEA-SMOOTH BONES IN FOURTEEN BROKEN ROWS

In your lizard-skin boots, reread the book of myths.
Dip it two parts whiskey to one part gunpowder.
Fall in tongues or fever, thieving the terrible.
Wake and feel the fell of dark, not day. What black hours.
Then saddle a sea horse and dive into the wreck.
Salvage all you can of the poets buried there.
Arrange their sea-smooth bones in fourteen broken rows.
Art is entrails spilled and a hand drawing itself.
Decide on a syllable count of twelve per line.
Carve out your space as the Cowgirl of Amour Fou
or the Cowboy of Ra rocking the Drunken Boat.
Employ a figure, a sidekick, to kick your ass.
Call him Murfy and take his advice: sonnetry
like shrapnel, like bricks through the living room window.

In The End We Walk The Long Tunnel, Dumb Slaughter

In the beginning was our bodies opening,
hip and gut pull to the bed springs of amour fou,
into second marriage after first divorces.
In the end we walk the long tunnel, dumb slaughter
for the knocking boxes. Kill pipe to body bag.
I want the final rending of my flesh from yours,
the taste of our blood in my teeth to know it's done.
I want the badges of damage for show-and-tell,
the bruises like fists blossoming under my skin,
I want, I want, but we both know I won't say it.
I'll stand like a wall, your face squeezing like knuckles,
and you won't leave a mark on me. I'll outwait you.
I wanted perfect space between us when we fought.
You want the perfect fight, film rewound past parents.

As If Lids Or Walls Kept Anything In Or Out

One room from the kill floor, your face knuckling into
mine, I curl inward like a slug or a body
or fingers in a fist, like liquor returning
to a jar as if there was safety in return,
as if lids or walls kept anything in or out,
as if the bottle was ever anything but
an analogy for our bag of skin, the neck
our neck, the body our body, the mouth our mouth,
the liquid the self we think is measurable,
containable, the container a glass body
bag, the full measure of who we are, a closed field,
our only escape a killing drain, a pouring
of our self into our self, a self-pitying
erasure, an annihilating inward curl.

MY UNTRANSLATABLE SIGNATURE BOMB SONNET

That first fuck you was hard to take. Then the second
like the flat head of a hammer bruising the wood
around a punched nail. Nothing negotiable.
Later, now, in the knuckling face of your anger,
the phrases you light and toss back like Molotovs,
shards peppering the air, I bottle resentment.
Tonight, with six fingers of bourbon blossoming
in my hothouse skull, I'll pull up the kill floor, leave
the marriage box through a trapdoor. I'll chase the noise
of my blood into the trees of repose, yawp word
and body, howl hundred-line rooftop bomb sonnets,
a yodel my untranslatable signature.
The bruises I'll wear like stories until they fade
and become baggage, old badges of my damage.

So I Send This Three-Word Burst, Poor Ink, Repeating

If I could load all I mean in metal casings,
in full jackets made to order, built from pictures
of my psyche, reverse time-lapse reconstruction
of the wreck to separate out the roots and shades,
a funneling back up out of the drain of self
in plosions of color streaking to the surface,
returned, called back, reunited, the sum of it,
all I mean, have ever meant, as if that could be
done in a word or a sonnet or a cartridge,
all of it loaded and locked like perfect meaning
in a magazine set to spray perfect bullets,
if I could, I would, but all I mean is too big,
too scattered, so I send this three-word burst, poor ink,
repeating: I want out, I want out, I want out.

MURFY THE BALLISTICIAN'S MUTINEER HOW-TO

Let me get this straight, Murfy says. What I call sea
you call drink, at the bottom of which lies the wreck
of self, the hull jangled and rocking like meaning
the morning after depth charges. So you said it.
You finally said yer three little words: I want out.
And here you are, rifling through maps and genius books
for a new word or route or the right note to bring
you to the surface of this tragic-gestured sea,
where you might intend a new world, articulate
an aesthetic of recovery and issue
a manifesto. My how-to for mutineers?
Find yer voice in yer roots. You want to break some bones,
use sticks and stones, but never forget yer first mate,
that most necessary of angels, gunpowder.

Happy Goddamn Goodbye Marriage Bottle Sonnet

I turn the apartment key on my awful wish:
the goodbye goddamn blank of nothing scrawled with threat,
no mirror lipsticked burn in hell, no sonnets smeared
in blood on the bed. No bed: clothes hangers, cardboard.
Here's the short list I can't erase like furniture
from a room: your voice, your face a fist through a wall,
my slamming doors and jumping from cars at stop signs,
my silence worse than bazookas, than getting beat
you said by your ex-husband in your seventh month,
that thing I used out of bed once like a brick: cunt.
Here's some stuff I can't find: rage, voice, that tequila
your friend gave me. I still can't drive a country road
and scream. Whassamatter white boy you said. Fuck you.
My plan: throw a bottle through the window. Begin.

ANOTHER DESPERADO TRACKING HIS ENTRAILS

Dear Diary, tonight, Tuesday, 20:35,
I'm a Winchester rifle strapped to a saddle
of distressed leather, another desperado
tracking his entrails like a hand drawing itself
in a cracked mirror, a leaking keg of powder
marking the way to Here in the County of There,
a spot on the road between Nohow and Nowhere.
Sunday, 1:57, here in the badlands,
this apartment of my latest false beginning,
the black flies and mosquitoes are big as grenades
and God's nothing but a bomb. Trapped in these four walls,
window cracked for air, I float in the tub and drink.
I nurse my pain one part gunpowder, two parts mash.
Somebody reads these words, say them like they're funny.

LAST NIGHT MY BED A BOAT OF WHISKEY GOING DOWN

My course last night no different: nailed to the bedroom
window frame a fitted sheet straining like a sail.
Collapsing like a lung. Rise and fall, rise and fall
of another night the same: my head a hammer
in the hold, a scribbling fist in the captain's log.
All this it seemed the same: the reluctant bachelor
and his bed a boat of whiskey tacking starboard
into the drink drank drunk he think thank thunk. And sunk.
This morning life's no ocean and this bed's not mired
in the drink of another low tide. I've neither
drifted from the mainstream nor washed ashore, flotsam
and jetsam like wrappers and butts. On the table
across the room a drum. Against the wall the books
are stacked like stacked books. Above the dresser a clock.

Making Like Scheherazade After The Smoke Clears

The way you've draped yourself on the couch and arranged
the evening like a still life: legs crossed like fingers,
twenty candles lit in broken rows on bookshelves,
a sheet tossed on the futon like a lover's shirt,
a bottle of wine and a third glass to your lips.
You'd almost think the Bat Phone is about to ring.
You predict sit-ups and sonnets and consider
having cards printed: Architect of the Hot Chance,
Mack Daddy, Cowboy Poet, Theorist of Desire.
You can't decide. Philosopher or Lizard King.
And you can't change the naked fact: that you're waiting
for something you can't name or find in hips alone.
You bluff your way through the night with diving stories
that tease the ocean floor and promise blue yonder.

UP FROM THE WRECK CONJURING MONTANA SONNET

No more diving into the wreck. From this point on,
move outward, over, through. Think prairie grass, badlands.
Think mountains. Trade your harpoon for a Remington.
Conjure Montana. Call it Buffalo Eden.
Give up the genius of the sea for the dark myth
of Tonto and the narrative of open fields,
but understand this first. Drawn tight as tom-tom skins,
you want the bang bang of it drumming like blood noise
in the rush of your loins to violence, though later
you'll deny the dumb animal grunt of it or,
worse, claim it comes from a dark place apart from you.
Tonto is the name we give to unchecked desire,
the place in us that understands dismemberment,
the open fields in us that resist narrative.

THESE ARCHAEOLOGIES OF SELF, THESE LIFE STUDIES

Tonight I'm the topographer of my desire.
No need for grace or wings lifting my boot-heeled feet
or any of the tired myths of sobriety.
My bed a map, I'm straddling pillows and blankets
like mountain chains, hurdling ridges, peaks, and mesas
like slurred words, a badlands sonneteer yodeling
and stumbling after Snodgrass through the universe.
At Whiskey Edge, I drink, watch the poets dig, scout
picks for the suicide pool. Serious business,
these archaeologies of self, these life studies.
I like the look of massacre when a poet
gives up sifting, strikes the last vault, the awful blood.
Confessing surfaces only, I stagger on,
the tinhorn poet of drink, see where it gets me.

WATCH THE HOT YOUNG WOMEN ON PURITAN BENCHES

How to deal with the long stretches, the distances
between the here and there of noway and nowhere.
A kitchen match on your lips, pick a role--Cowgirl
of Ra or Cowboy of Amour Fou--and play it.
Watch the hot young women on puritan benches
squeezing and calling the shots. Sip mash from your flask
like you're nitrogen cool, about to blow and beat
the tom-tom skins, like you can bang bang the blood straight
from the rush of violence through to animal grunt.
Make a joke about the Lizard King and snaky
Medusa being the same hothouse garden whore.
Then one half-beat before your cue, their puritan
hips moving, hair twisting, perform the myth of boots
and denim cowboy hard on their big sky mattress.

FOURTEEN-GALLON COWBOY FULL OF MASH AND SWAGGER

A string of publications in the right places
and, bingo, an invitation to a dinner
for poets. You're hard to miss in your ankle-length
duster, lizard-skin boots, and fourteen-gallon hat
iridescent as birthday cellophane. Dogie,
not dawgie, you tell them. Full of mash and swagger,
you say things like Cowboy Word Up. They go crazy.
You do a rope trick. They sway like targets. You mark
your turf: bazooka sonnetry, liquor and love.
You roll into the butter, rock the gravy boat.
Two things confirm you're drunk: Language poet Tonto
and his editor Annie Oakley love your work,
and Texas Slam Poet winks Redneck Lit Power
and you don't shoot him for misunderstanding you.

Yodel's What I Call The Uncontainable Noise

Understand the fixed syllable count, twelve per line,
and the fourteen lines plus the fifteenth, the title,
not as shrine, but as a spell or a fist squeezing
the center of nothing gathering. Never facts,
only interpretations. And the next bullet.
What you'd expect: the architecture of sonnets
plaster castings of entrails spilled and hands drawing
themselves, not that the drawing or spilling itself
is any more real or less solid than castings.
What are badges of damage after all but words
or records we make of the bruising? The yodel's
what I call the uncontainable noise I bring,
drunk, to all of this annihilating inward
and the red weather of the open fields I cross.

Say She's On Top Tossing The Moon Back Like A Shot

Say you're drunk and knee deep in theories of desire,
stereo cranked, and you know better than bourbon
what the thumping means, the violence under your skin
like noise in a drum, like Tonto caught in his name.
You know all about the absent object, how lack
motors desire and bodies seek dismemberment.
Say Annie Oakley's on top tossing the moon back
like a shot of vodka, and you make the mistake
of calling yourself the architect of rapture.
You're a poet, she says. Think Bacchus. Better spells
than shrines if you're talking hairy fist of werewolf
gathering at the center of nothing squeezing.
Otherwise your sonnets are blank shells, body bags,
and you're no cowboy of drunken love poetry.

Like Paint Bullets Exploding, Annie O Hits Me

Throwing spells at the phone like dice, I drink and wait
for Oakley to call about that tour with Tonto,
a murderous poetry spree across the West.
Bang! At ten the door and sharp-shooting Annie O.
My art, she says, is a kind of action painting.
I fire these plastic bullets at things that take paint.
Canvases, boards, buildings, animals with thick hides.
How about the moon, I whisper. She slides her hand
down my washboard belly. I done roped that dogie,
even shot it once, but I understand your need.
You're a poet. The moon's important. So let's deal.
I'll drive us all to Tulsa. I have some work there.
Later, the untranslatable. Like paint bullets
exploding, she hits me. I do my best werewolf.

Godless Murfy Has His Say About Massacre

So this is it, yer in love again, Murfy says.
Hope has you by the short hairs or yer heart-shaped heart
or something even more sentimental, like moons
or prairie blossoms. Something about those four walls
that mock the body, the bottle, the body bag,
that close a man or a woman like a fixed field,
that invite a prison break, a tunneling out
of the self, say, in the spring, or maybe out west,
after which you'll flow to an old country yodel.
A few things first, though. There is no outside of time
in drunken love, however untranslatable.
Some of her baggage is massacre. That dark place,
it's not in you, it's of you, and she's no different.
There's a story in Tulsa you don't want to hear.

MURFY BLESSES THE COWBOY OF DRUNKEN LOVE'S LOVE

Here's some stuff from last night, Cowboy. Lizard-skin moon.
Boots black. That long-finned Cadillac convertible
Oakley loaned you and Tonto outside of Tulsa.
On the hood the shrunken head of Wallace Stevens
bobbing like a compass thinking west. Accident
she said. Liquor and love make corpses of us all.
Poetry's the taxidermy of red weather.
Taxidermy's the poetry of body bags.
That much you can remember. And down the highway
Tonto calling the shots, the cigarettes flicking
like fireflies, and bodies scattering like empties.
This isn't the way you planned it. So there's no God
and things have a way of turning to massacre.
The good news is frontier. Baggage is part of it.

My Prairie Love Blossoms In Wildflower Sonnets

Here's where drink gets me. Over mountains and badlands,
across fields, back to prairie grass. Unrepentant.
My suitcases unloaded in sequence and stacked
on the porch like cartridges, a Remington's length
from the whiskey barrel that has my name on it.
Here's the April scene. Oakley pointing at the moon,
saying the rivers in me are dark and lyric.
I call her a prairie blossom, a cornflower.
A crack shot, she adds. I nod, and the wolves kick in,
their ludic choir yawping epithalamium.
Sounds good, she says, and we drink to frontier in us
and out, the baggage part of it. Scars are stories,
she says. Or poems, I add. Our plan: handfasting
to a sour-mash yodel, things flowing as they will.

O'KEEFFE AND STEVENS

Georgia And Wallace Drive To Holy Ghost, Illinois

They met at somebody's house. There was a thunderstorm
loud as rockets. The power went off just like that. Click.
When it came back on, they were driving north to Holy Ghost.
First-marriage boxes in the back of somebody's truck. Something
old and borrowed. She was driving. The road map was new.
Nothing was blue, so he kept repeating the same line,
something about the blue river of truth. He said that's what
they were taking to their new home. It curled, he said,
through the firm ground of fiction. She shifted in her seat
and looked at a field scattered with cows like dumb luggage.
She said how do you know that? How does anyone know that?
He said he read it in a book. He didn't know why it had to be blue.

WALLACE AND GEORGIA PERFORM THEIR LOVE IN TREES

Outside of Holy Ghost, down this road, across that field,
just off the blue river of truth, is a creek bed she discovered
on one of her walks. It was an afternoon quiet as a closet.
Now they take their love outside. It's come to that.
As she thinks color and light, perspective and angle,
he brushes twigs from her back, considers them props
in their fall amphitheater, discards a half-formed line,
starts another. The hands he's using to wash her thighs
as she rolls into the lip of water are, like her hips, he says,
key players in this ancient ceremony. He talks like that.
Then in the light fluting through the leaves, they perform
their love, her belly flattening in the wet sand, his knees
hitting their mark, her long back arching like rising action,
their movements plot devices, narrative seductions
for delaying the inevitable denouement, when the ache
of geometry chases ambition from the dream of their bodies
and they drop away at familiar angles, muscles returning.
And as always, as it never is indoors among the maps,
the marriage boxes, a gust rattles the trees in applause.

Georgia And Wallace Move West And Argue About Flowers

She's caught again.
An old argument
about flowers.
Not, she says, the idea
of a world only, but more the world itself
opening and closing. In her mind,
yes, but out there as well. Out there
Black Petunia & White Morning-Glory,
Banana Flower, Yellow Sweet Peas.
He's mounting the same
attack, raking over the same
ground, killing everything.
Your Sunflower, he says,
takes dominion, tames New Mexico.
Your Calla Lilies raise church walls.
Your Red Canna, backlit with glory,
is the first pulse, more red weather
than flower. More pudenda
than you will ever admit.
She's becoming her work, Cow's Skull
with Calico Roses filling a hole
in her portfolio. He's this room, she tells herself.
An airless chamber. A marriage box.
Nothing small about those flowers, he says.
Poems of rapture and rupture, he says.
She thinks. A dry summer and a desire,
a memory of paint and the fact
of flowers. That more
than the idea of them.
Petunia and Choleus.
Calla Lily with Red Roses.
Nicotina.

WALLACE AND GEORGIA MAKE LIKE MONSTERS OVER NEW MEXICO

Wallace smashes a glass and rises, Eight-Forked Serpent of Koshi,
over Ghost Ranch, New Mexico. Each morning he sucks
the bones of another maiden dry.

Georgia rides men all night over Chama River Valley. Hag of moons
and crossroads, she straddles their broomstick hips.
They drop in Swallow Pond.

Eight-headed, eight-tailed Wallace casts a noon shadow over eight hills
and valleys before pouring another tub of beer
and settling down to write.

Boulders tumbling from her smock, mountains forming, Georgia lands
on her pueblo rooftop and sees the single red flower
in the dry arroyo that needs her.

GEORGIA AND WALLACE MARK DEPTH IN A DRY SUMMER

Like carpenters
dropping a plumb
in an old house
or barge mates
marking depth
in a dry summer,
they knew what
they'd find:
nothing's square
or ever will be
or deep enough
and said as much
every time they said
something else.

Wallace and Georgia
are run aground tonight
by vague desire,
something about a hole in a map.
Wallace's lashed to the couch
by the words
he's spat in this room.
Georgia's crackling,
a bank of embers on the shore,
this room a corked bottle,
her tongue the note inside.
They're run aground tonight
by vague desire,
something about the memory
of their words,
not the words themselves,
nor the things
they catch in their teeth
and tear,
but something

about something to say
lost to them now,
something about these charts
and maps in the box
at their feet.

WALLACE AND GEORGIA GO FOR THEIR GUNS

Something sparked it. A lamp broke.
Coyote came in through the window.
Scorpion fell into the gravy bowl.

She stretched a canvas too tight,
and later when the frame snapped,
it was the perfect excuse.

All those flowers made Wallace sneeze.
He could never get comfortable.
The chairs were made of cow skulls.

Ghost Ranch was Georgia's.
He blocked the light, talked too much.
Hard to tell who threw the first shot.

Georgia And Wallace Plead With The Seven Angels Of Confusion

They want it declared more than a befuddlement,
more than just another bad can of marriage worms.
For the record, Georgia believes in light and colors
and lines and her position before Sunrise and Little Clouds.
She climbs the ladder to the roof, stretches a canvas,

snaps the house in two. After one of his twenty-mile walks,
Wallace sinks heavy like melons, bits of argument caught
in the cuffs of his pants, phrases curling in his hair.
He pours a drink and eats the bottle. Wallace and Georgia
want their marriage ruled an abomination, an incoherence.

They want it made indispensable, rolled in the serpents
of long memory, recorded in the Book of Monsters,
so they call on the Seven Angels of Confusion to do
the last violence for them. To bring it to a head.
To use their tricks of distortion to wage a public campaign

for immortality. Wallace's standing before a mirror
in his closed-off room. He's thinking about poetry.
He's rising above the house, darkening the hills
and canyons. Georgia's finishing the painting
she's been working on for weeks. In it she and Wallace

kneel among the Seven Angels to make their awful case.
In it, foreground right, Bigtha and Abatha, Winepressers,
are taking a break, sharing a cigarette and a look
as they listen. Barbonah the Annihilator, top left, shaded,
is killing something. Hard to tell what. Behind Wallace

and Georgia, left of center, a pile of demons hacked
to pieces. Carcas, Knocker of Things Possible,
and Bitztha the Housewrecker are rooting in the pile,
arranging pieces on a white plate, on a gold chain.
Their heads are cocked, favoring their good ears.

In it the fingers of Georgia and Wallace are lit
to show the blood, to make the basic narrative connection.
To say the hacking's their handiwork. Wallace and Georgia
don't look good. Pieces of them seem to be missing.
To suggest another connection. To raise the possibility

the demons were theirs. Though only a few of the letters
are visible, it's clear the exhibits arrayed before
Zethar, Observer of Immorality, and Mehuman, Confusion Itself,
run from A to Z. Georgia and Wallace enter their plea
directly to these two, make their case for dissolution.

In his marriage box, Wallace drinks and writes a poem
about Georgia and Wallace. In it they're sentenced
to an unspecified belly, written up in the Book of Monsters,
disappeared in cannibal marriage. Joint by joint. Piece
by piece. Wallace by Georgia by Wallace. Mythy stuff.

WALLACE AND GEORGIA DRINK OUTSIDE A BOWLING ALLEY

Rock and rye, two glasses,
back of her pickup. Tuesday
Women's League. Wallace
kicks a longneck from under
a tire because, he says, it's
come to that, kicking a bottle
to save a tire. Georgia's raw

tonight. But for what got
the rub there, she says,
I could be any rodeo angel
holding a ten-pound swirly ball
five steps from a Vodka Collins
and another split nail. Pulling
cans of beer from a cooler,

she flaps her arms and rises,
balancing on the tailgate.
Not sting of flesh, he says,
makes you special or the pubis
that put it there, or your pubis
grinding back, but paint lit
with redemption. Now it's

pudenda flowers to fit a canvas
and what you trade for your fill
of women, their salty minutes.
Not fill, she says, but taking
my Sappho measure, and not the tip
of my tongue if that's what
you're asking. Further back's

the glory. You'll see when she
gets here. If it all works out.
The three of us. Ghost Ranch.

She loves your mind. Wallace rises
beside Georgia, two fingers
of absinthe to his temple, glass
pressed hard. They bounce

for hours under the light outside
Red Sky Lanes, drinking the liquor
they've loaded in the back
of her pickup, brought here
to the wall of spectacular endings
for one final jackknife
off the tailgate, the last act

they'll play out in their theater
of the needful for anyone who
might be watching, poet and
painter landing, gravel
crunching under their boots
like lights-up after last call,
hard truth.

GEORGIA AND WALLACE UNDO THEIR BUNDLE OF HISS

It's the noise they make together
that gets them. Alone she flaps
like white laundry in a dry wind.
He's his favorite pair of pants
clipping through the low brush
or his resoled shoes scuffing
the gravel of a county road.
The noise they make together
is the bundle of hiss they undo,
the snakes they pull apart.

WALLACE AND GEORGIA REPRISE AN OLD STANDARD

The ending you might expect.
Mattress in the middle of a room.
Divorce boxes. Books.
Bottle and glass on the floor.
A clock.

Noise the room makes
in aftermath is white.

ANOTHER YODEL

A HUNDRED-LINE ROOFTOP SOUR-MASH YODEL SONNET

The Lost Yodel Sonnets were never really lost
but left under the wreck, twisting in the roots
and shades not far from the bones of poets
who preceded me there, terrible
jangling of holds ripped and spilling
the entrails of words and maps,
a puzzle of black hours
and metal casings
for those of us
who salvage
what we
can,
our
flashlights

waving through
the fell of dark,
as we fall
and rise
to the bottom
of things,
where we study
the captain's log,
scattered,
pages missing,
as if
it could be made complete
with the dumb
hope of pilgrims

and a manifesto:
this is it,
this is ours,
this is what
we've come
to pick through,
recover,

repack
to find our voice.
Which,
in my case,
means howl
or scrawl
or cowboy yawp,

means bricks and bullets
or sonnets rupturing
like body bags,
tom-tom skins,
like the thump
of the blood
or the jump
in our guts,
the pull
of the absent object
or Bacchus blowing
the walls off
a closed field,
means bazookas

launched
like rapture
from rooftops,
that which is
finally uncontainable:
perfect noise:
untranslatable:
always drunk:
a pouring
in and out:
body
to bottle
to sonnet:
my terrible trinity

always threatening
the next jail break. Under
the sea wreck, the Lost Yodel

Sonnets, waving, do their work. Up
here, we live our lives, for the most part,
horizontally, the far lines marking
appearances, suggesting boundaries, blocking
a scene, framing a canvas or a page
or a sonnet, the limits that make
massacre inevitable,
the necessary angel.
Up here, we monitor
the lines that set one
green field off from

another,
loosen
the
tension
between the
air of yonder
and the dirt of here.
What I see now is flow,
everything always melting,
the wolves erasing the walls we
put up. Here on the porch, on the roof,
handfasting in the yard with Annie O,
paint bullets and sour-mash yodels making this
territory the undefinable something
we agree on, I've learned a few things. We live in time,
but out of step. We drink, howl rivers, shoot prairie blossoms.

ALL THIS TUG

Zoo Story

You know the story about the couple.
Any color, any neighborhood.
Growled and snapped at each other,
slept in balls of fur and hunger,
stalked necessity, cornered chance,
ate the weak. Humped for years
like clockwork. Usual lion stuff.
Simple as that.

Nothing, as you know, is simple as that.
Clocks wind down. Batteries go dead.
That's the way with time.
One day the lions assume the position,
the one that's worked for years,
and the humping goes all to hell.
One of them, take your pick,
is dreaming monkey love.

The trees and all that falling
from limb to loin
in the carnival of hips and hands?
Old as feet, that story.
The one who can't imagine the branches?
Net or stray bullet or sleep-tipped dart.
That ending. The one who can?
Happily, they say, ever after.

1. Split screen. Her sink's clogged with roots, she tells Cowboy on the phone. She pulls and pulls in her dream. For balance and a better angle, she climbs and straddles the sink. I had a dream about this, Cowboy says bottom right. In it you're straddling and pulling and straddling and the only thing you're wearing is a baggy tee shirt. Let me guess, she says. You rise from the drain on a miracle stallion, roots hanging from your lance like kelp or my tee shirt. I don't talk like that, he says. If anything, you brought me there, conjured me up through the pipes. My hero, she sighs, my very own roto-rooter cowpoke come to dig me out, cut me free to what end?

Cut to subjective shot up through roots. At her ankles, calves, Cowboy checks his bearings by touch, by smell, and rises like the morning sun. Iris to black and back to light.

2. He squints. The sun's hard at three o'clock. A forest forty miles from here, she says, where people go with red wine and loaves of thick bread to write their love poetry. No fill or back lighting, Cowboy's leaning to cast a longer shadow. Cordoned off by the state, it's posted with signs like little poems chattering to themselves, like footnotes explicating a canopy of oak and elm, a bed of picnic table and barbecue, like charts anatomizing a working model veined with trails, valved with gates. Cowboy clears his throat. Means one thing only, something he read once: thinking chaos, thinking fences. Maybe late tomorrow morning, she says, away from the trash cans and hand rails, somewhere under an emulous sky, blue and cupped, a clearing. He squints, lights a smoke with a kitchen match. Background, the bang banging of tom-tom skins. Cut. Black.

3. The set requires Cowboy's attention. Pears and a red pepper in a blue bowl. Cheese on a cutting board and/or thick bread. Table wine, always table wine. Red. Daisies or a tulip in a jelly jar. Never a rose. A few books, Neruda, Duras, Barthes, maybe some cowboy love poetry, by the bowl. Blue bowl. Newspaper opened to the arts

section, puzzle begun. One pencil. Coffee brewing. Outside, if possible, rain. On the stereo, something high and lonesome by Hank Williams or anything by Billie Holiday or Edith Piaf or Patsy Cline. Sunday morning adultery, Cowboy knows, is an art like waiting for his next scene.

4. So they had one last talk late one night over the phone. What's it about, she said, this poem. Cowboy cleared the rattler from his throat, a leather strop, the handsaw he'd swallowed to build their Bitterroot cabins one stone's throw apart. About lovers, he said, making love three days straight. Woman wrote it, he said. Knocked mud out of his boots off the back porch like he was in a movie. It was a portable phone.

It wasn't her husband, she said. I'm not your husband, he said. Coughed up some barbwire, gunpowder, a scorpion. Poured himself a drink. And, she asked, are you sure she used the word love. Sure dark as flop out here, he said. You're a regular cowboy poet, she said. Cowboy drank that straight to Whiskey Edge, this side of Plunge.

5. Grainy like the film's been drug over cactus. Everything lit for shadows. In the foreground, bottle, glass, six-shooter. Rack focus to the cowboy brim behind it all and the new woman walking into the frame. Cool as snake nerve. Still as the long pause before the first hand drops, goes for it, slaps leather. Hoka-hey, Cowboy. It's a good day to die.

Credits roll.

HOLY GHOST BUILDING 1995

Seventh Sunday after Easter, what the preachers
call Pentecost, and here we sit, we Men of the Book,
jiggling our feet, shaking the table like disciples hot

for their usual: descent of spirit, Jesus breath biting
at the back of our necks, and the promise of tongues.
Ninety years after the Azusa Street Revival in the City

of Angels, California, where modern Pentecostalism
was born, we're holding our ecumenical service here
in downtown Champaign, Illinois, at our favorite corner

church, the Esquire Lounge, serving food and spirits to People
of the Book. Our Books of Hale and her Godey's Lady's Book,
of Swift and Anglo-Irish Ascendancy, of Holy Keith Hernandez

and Baseball Televised in Bars. Our Books of Walker
and American Imperialist Psalms, of Acker and Ecofeminism
Eat God, of Kerouac and Last Call in Zen Heaven.

We're doing the best we can with the Women of the Book gone,
lost to new pulpits, not schisms or apostasy. The three of us left
to our own devices, the chant of Scotch, Rum, Bourbon

our Father, Son, Ghost, and the passing of the collection plate
and another round of drinks we fetch from the u-shaped bar
we pretend looks like a cross--all this, all these

the long tease before rapture. Our little table the tent I need
for the full-gospel revival I'm leading tonight. I see
the Foursquare Brass Rail across the way and talk about

Sister Aimee Semple McPherson's vision and what she made
of Ezekiel's in 1:4-14, how she saw in the four swirling shapes
the four faces, the cornerstones of Christ's ministry,

his holy ghost building: savior, healer, baptizer, king. I tell them
around the corner's the Restoration Urban Ministries that used
to be a porn theater back in the sixties. I make

no jokes about the visions folks must be having there. Except
this one: A man walks into a church with a parrot in his pants.
The bartender says, "That a sign of the resurrection

or you just happy to see me?" I tell my brothers about the spirit
that will drop from the ceiling later, settle at our table,
and find its voice in us, in spirit baptism,

the Pentecostal flame licking up our thighs. Tonight my sermon's
glossolalia, that jangling choir, the red hot hallelujah
of healing Azusa Street pouring from shot glasses.

ATHENSVILLE, ILLINOIS

Her mother said write whereabouts
unknown if prison's too hard a word
to write on a nursing-school application.

Not the way I would have told that part
of her story. For driving the wrong hogs
to the wrong market, that little piggy,

drunken hog-thief piggy, had to go
is what I would have put down. Or
in the weeds he squats, tells her to tell

her mother to take him back. He'll slice
his stomach open if she doesn't. That one.
Years later, four children of her own,

daughter kills the liquor on his breath
with threat of no family. He becomes
a good man who did a few bad things,

then dies fifteen years later. In a box,
a Prince Albert can, crimp cut. Does Not
Bite The Tongue. Two bar chips, each 10¢

in trade. Astroth Tav. 602 Belle St.
Jack & Donna Tavern. Hettick, Ill.
From his year in the service, a nickel

notebook of poker numbers, a sailor ditty,
and this line: Jan 15, 1939, got the clap.
Story I'd tell ends that way. No talk of cure.

My Mountain Price 1

After the dark and the tug in all kinds of weather, marriage weather, divorce weather, death weather, drunken cowboy weather, I sit here and name my mountain price.

I bring it all this far, the baggage I haul because it's mine to haul.

Two failed marriages. Usual history of family drink. Babies born in bushes between Pennsylvania and central Illinois rural. Hillbillies come north from southeast Missouri to the Illinois side of St. Louis to work refineries, canals. Hartford smell of oil and earth and tannery in my blood. Burning cross, madness, prison dangling from one family branch. Murder and suicide from the other. Preachers collecting on both.

My father died last month. I carry that news in a paper bag, an open bottle. Ain't no hill, he'd say, for a high-stepper. I repeat his happy lie here at the table so there's no misunderstanding. The hills are mountains.

They set the value I place on all I've carried this far, the good and the bad, inseparable from the voice I bring it in, loud as cowboy hats and lizard-skin boots.

It's here at Whiskey Edge, all this tug, the dark lifting, in bourbon-soaked cowboy love poems, I name my mountain price.

HARTFORD, ILLINOIS

In the one tattooed on my right forearm, your father's
father, my father, born 1930, rides a blue ox
and picks his teeth with railroad ties. On the back

of my neck, I wear the union brand: leather boot,
a fist, and a company truck tipped over and burning
like a chip on my father's father's right shoulder. On

my left arm, over that same shoulder, his shoulder,
some men knocking a shack together and signs
to tell their story. It's 1933. They're talking union

on the tracks this side of the International Shoe
Tannery property line. Your father's father,
my father, worked as a Shell Oil pipefitter

a mile east, other side of the Tannery, before retiring,
1983, a Shell company man in Louisiana. On strike
in 1962 he took me, your father, born 1954, to a union

shack at midnight. We slept outside in the back
of our station wagon. Today the Tannery's a vacant
Shell property, and Hartford's burning on my skin

like the ground under 507 N. Olive, my birth home,
Hartford dirt soaked with decades of product
piped from White Star, Sinclair, Standard, Roxana,

Shell, Clark, Premcor, carried over and piped under
the tracks laid by the Big-4 and the CP&StL,
to the canal, the barges, and the confluence,

Mississippi and Missouri, that attracted Lewis
and Clark in December 1803. Here, it's May 1998,
my father's still alive, and he's inking a final

two-frame tattoo on my chest. In it, first frame,
my father's father's telling his friend Tennessee,
journeyman boxer turned union buster, to take

his boys and leave, that if he, Tennessee, takes
one more step, puts boot to the next tie, he,
my father's father, will kill him with his hands

right there. In the second frame, Tennessee's
telling that story to my father, who's telling
his kid brother, born 1946, who's telling me

so I'll tell you. Like movie dialogue. Tennessee
didn't want to die that day. It's what I have
to work with, to explain my skin to you. We're

all there, 1933, on the Tannery tracks talking
union. Our arms are like hams, our waists
thirty inches, and we can stop a man

with our eyes. There's a Hartford tattoo
on my father's belly, deep in the skin. It's 1973.
The scene's a sidewalk, northeast corner Delmar

and Elm. The Tomlovic son's washing the family
crime, our crime, blood and brains of a shotgun
murder-suicide off the walls of his family's store,

the first store built in Hartford, incorporated
in 1920. My father grew up on Elm, just over
the tracks. The Tannery was built in 1916.

My father was a union man, Plumbers &
Pipefitters Local 553, Wood River, and then
he wasn't. I used to work at Peavey Flour Mill,

later talked Marxism at a private college,
hung IWW posters on my office walls.
My father's father died when my father

was eleven. My father never got the tattoo
he wanted, the one in which his favorite cousin
did not kill his wife and then himself. My father

could not stop family history. Next year he
will die unexpectedly. Hartford burns on my
skin, inks these tattoos I give you, my daughter.

Married a carpenter who stretched canvases. I tried my hand at paint but feared the white space. One day she built a door and walked through it.

Married a rain forest but tired of its threats, the match to its head, the gasoline in my lungs. One day I coughed up a bomb, blew off an arm.

In the badlands I opened a store. There I learned supply and demand, terrain and weather, drank the profit I could afford.

In the mountains, I learned guns, became a preacher, wrote jeremiads, loved the hard lesson, regrew that arm.

That was before I met the sharpshooter on the blue horse. She tossed some coins in the collection plate and took me home.

1.

Brooklyn, June 1995, fourth-floor Berkeley Place, Park Slope walk-up, front window, where Cowboy arranges himself with props.

Viz., book, pen, binoculars, repeating rifle, and postcard of a nude man in profile against a black background, light sheeting down his back and what you'd never call his perfect ass because you leave the dirty work to Cowboy, the dismembering of bodies, the grading and cataloguing of parts.

Behind the nude man and before him, circles and wheels and cable connecting all.

Cowboy sits in the window, ex-wife and her wife and their roommate, the gay actor, all facing him from the couch, watching tv as he watches the street.

During commercial, they notice the card in his hand, the beautiful naked man, the circles and wheels and cable.

They nod, make jokes about the closet door creaking open.

Ex-wife points to the way Cowboy fingers the card, the way he's always fingered pens, binoculars, books, rifles, flatware, linen.

And probably, she adds, when she wasn't looking, Doctor, Lawyer, Baker, Thief, and Village People Indian Chief.

Cowboy hears the laugh track and feels the pull down through the trees to the street, back across the country, back to central Illinois corn, where you'll read and reread the one-word poem above the man, Desire, the circles, the wheels, the cable, the naked body, all of it roped with a word to set a value, this postcard your beautiful naked man rain check.

2.

Cowboy sits in a bar window, early lunch of beer, shepherd's pie, now coffee.

Outside's Washington Square and the NYU Cowboy Poetry Conference he's escaped.

Inside's Counter Guy polishing a glass and Waitress putting white napkins on brown tables.

Outside Manhattan's belly to brain, gut to leg, a thousand tongues and arms going at once.

Inside Cowboy's hunched over a full cup and a Statue of Liberty post-card the size of his chest, scribbling and sketching for you the rest of his day, his itinerary, which begins with the lover's heart pulled and rising above the city like King Kong at high noon or Man Ray's float-ing lips.

Cowboy watches Waitress light a candle, looks out the window.

Cowboy writes another line, something about somewhere over Ohio or Indiana, corn field this, bean field that, the heart taking on weight, a torso, then the bodies of poets, living and dead, tucked like books under the arms it sprouts.

Counter Guy muffles a cough, and Cowboy looks out the window, then to the door, half-expecting the plot disturbance to walk in, belly to brain, gut to leg, some five-foot Rizzo grab him by the arm and teach him big-city ropes, play Ratso to his hayseed flaneur.

Cowboy looks out the window as Waitress fills his cup.

Outside in Brooklyn's the Park Slope street fair where yesterday Cowboy bought the earrings for you, the ones in his pocket.

Inside today's the Statue of Liberty postcard and Cowboy drawing the pockets on the pants around the legs the naked torso takes on,

Cowboy's legs, Cowboy's feet, his boots, as he crosses, descending into Illinois with the funny story he'll tell you about what he said at the cheese table to the ten-gallon poet.

Inside today's a cowboy postcard poem about the lover's heart, the beast in his cowboy belly, the pull of his cowboy loins, the same old unlocatable lover's urge to the white picket fences of forever this, children, and happy endings that.

Out there's all of it by four o'clock.

MEAT-AXE BEDTIME STORY FOR GROWN PRAIRIE DAUGHTERS

That marriage can be a set of flight patterns, a map of yonder, the bag on your back, one neurectomy after another, the twin faces of tragedy and comedy and the third mask.

That the thing between your legs, like your nose and your ears and your belly button and your feet, needs the light of a name, a word signifying power, sovereignty, like a flag over land you control.

That liquor and love, badly lived, keep a mean ledger.

That the third mask is your take, your riff, your phrasing, your untranslatable something.

That family is an old spiritual about a holy ghost building and all of us are carpenters of the air.

That cunt is a fist, a hand, the tragic-gestured sea, a paint bullet splashing, a Georgia O'Keeffe flower, Man Ray's floating lips, the lover's heart.

That there is always baggage.

That my nightmare inventory won't and will be yours.

That you're the swing of the hammer, the trajectory of the bullet or the spray.

That cock is a handlebar, a pinkie finger, a bottle rocket, a rooster crowing, a rose painted on the side of a ship, King Kong, the lover's heart.

That the perimeters of family can't be mapped.

That desire is the open field.

That you will write your own hundred-line yodel sonnets.

That Meat-Axe Day is a bedtime story about the lengths to which lovers, friends, and family will go to lop off our pain, the heaviness of unwant and disease, their hard love the axe, the hatchet, the tomahawk.

CENTRAL ILLINOIS CORN

When my father died,
that was my hard time,
my head a cave of winds.

This is my easy time,
our prairie daughters riding
their mother's blue horse

through the far bean fields
and all this central Illinois
corn. Happy ending.

LAST YODEL

ANOTHER HUNDRED-LINE DRUNKEN COWBOY SONNET

Poetry's led me here, this far:
rethink the ocean floor:
trunks of pirate treasure,
necessary as red weather,
unearthed near the wreck,
brought to the surface,
up the ladder, onto the schooner,
crowbarred: metal casings,
gunpowder, bottles, bricks,
sticks, a single bazooka,
and pieces of a thousand
thousand Lost Yodel Sonnets:
Here's the scene at Annie O's
A RHETORIC OF RAPTURE AND RUPTURE SONNET
More than thirteen ways Murfy says of making a
Frenzy Dismemberment Bacchus
From the dark place, the Other in you understood
as desire packed and rolled in a theory you can
explain, a trophy you can dangle from your pony
yer self-pitying sonnet blather
And back always a pouring in and
The throwaway country line liquor and love make
Your journey will make more sense if you understand
Whassamatter white boy you
YOU'RE SUCH A BASTARD YOU BASTARD DIVORCE SONNET
genius pages drifting wrapping around
Ethnicity Absent Object
Erotic because taboo, empowering because
it marks moments of rebellion, autonomy,
because mutinous (cunt: she who refuses twice)
your myths. Tonto's the name you give your savagery bomb
ROOSTER CROWING ROSE AND BOTTLE ROCKET SONNET
Blood in the water like smoke like gestures
these nightmare measurements of masculine worth
bleeding through lines sign of death health sign of all signs
GEORGIA O'KEEFFE WAS JUST PAINTING FLOWERS SONNET
Say hairtrigger tigers in really red weather
ten times. Say you hit delete and start all over

CACOPHONY MOUNTAINS AREN'T HIGH ENOUGH SONNET
DEEP AS THE WRECK AND PUSHING UP DAISIES SONNET
something apart from you, you know it's in you
The I of all this first-person declarative
or exclamatory insisting
She takes your left hand and puts it between
Across a table, against a wall, through a door
cock, cocking, cocked
MAN RAY'S FLOATING LIPS UP AND KISS KING KONG SONNET
in my bourbon dreams
and halfway through the sonnet
and halfway through the sonnet
SOMETHING YOU CAN PUT IN YOUR PIPE AND SMOKE SONNET
Your first wife and her wife and
History throws need on a potter's wheel and works it
into desire
I'm the one at the table a little too loud
RAS THE DESTROYER EXHORTING TONTO SONNET
A maze ain't a maze if you can find yer way out
like it was
piss and yawp and howl and scrawl and
FELL OF DARK ANOTHER PHRASE I'VE STOLEN SONNET
but if you don't give folks a way out it's nothing
but a wall folding in on itself like entrails
and if that's what yer going to do you better
have pretty pictures to look at along the way
AIN'T NO WAY YOU'LL SHOOT YER WAY OUT OF HERE SONNET
gin and bourbon and beer and wine and vodka and
HOLY GHOST HOLY COW TALKING IN TONGUES SONNET
TIME GETS WEIRD AND THERE'S NO DAMN WHERE TO GO SONNET
FREAKING FOR NO PARTICULAR REASON SONNET
Call it everything I've been aiming, shooting for,
call it the white picket fences of forever,
call it my lot in life, the burden I'll carry
like bags of feed from truck to mouth, the July
fields where Annie O and I hope to sow our seed,
the babies we're planning to birth and raise under
a godless sky, in the open space of no myth
or a book of new myths, all of it bleeding like
MEAT-AXE DAY AND NIGHT TILL YOU GET IT RIGHT SONNET
But it doesn't have to be that way, Murfy says
NOT IF YOU KEEP TO THE GOOD STUFF COWBOY SONNET

and remember what's important that the family
you come from had arms like hams and eyes that could kill
a man and you love your perfect parents sisters
and the women were strong and bad whiskey passed like
PASSED LIKE ONE LAST HARD PISS OFF THE BACK PORCH SONNET
And the family you're building with me, Annie says,
isn't a building, isn't a bottle, its neck
your neck, its mouth your mouth, its body your body.
The family you're building with me is a yodel
jumping with blood noise, liquor through my veins, rivers
howling, drunken boats shooting rapids like rapture
YER BLOOD NOISE THUMPS GUT TO LEG LIKE CRAZY SONNET
YOUR BLOOD NOISE IS THE NOISE BANGING MY HEART SONNET
MY BLOOD NOISE IS THE WILD VOICE IN YOUR EYES SONNET
OUR WILD VOICES COME SCREAMING TOGETHER SONNET
COMING TOGETHER LIKE HOLLYWOOD UR-SONNET
What we'll drink to:
handfasting forever this:
happy endings that.

A Note on the Notes

A willingness to satisfy contradictory objections to one's manner of writing, might turn one's work into the donkey that finally found itself being carried by its masters, since some readers suggest that quotation-marks are disruptive of pleasant progress; others, that notes to what should be complete are a pedantry or evidence of an insufficiently realized task. But since in *Observations*, and in anything I have written, there have been lines in which the chief interest is borrowed, and I have not yet been able to outgrow this hybrid method of composition, acknowledgements seem only honest. Perhaps those who are annoyed by provisos, detainments, and postscripts, could be persuaded to take probity on faith and disregard the notes.

Marianne Moore
(*Collected Poems*, 1951)

Note on No Notes

This book jimmies a few lids and doors to borrow a phrase here and there. If probity on faith is impossible and notes you must, then ask and I'll give up sources. I took no oath.

Steve Davenport
dvnprt@gmail.com
(for playgiarism complaints)

69